IF I GET HIT
BY A BUS
TOMORROW,

HERE'S *How To*
REPLACE THE
Toilet Paper **ROLL**

Published by Willow Creek Press
P.O. Box 147, Minocqua, Wisconsin 54548

For information on other Willow Creek Press titles,
call 1-800-850-9453

Printed in The United States of America

IF I GET HIT BY A BUS TOMORROW,

HERE'S *How To* REPLACE THE *Toilet Paper* ROLL

A WOMAN'S INSTRUCTIONAL *Guide* FOR MEN

By MARY MCHUGH

WILLOW CREEK PRESS

CONTENTS

INTRODUCTION

I've noticed a strange phenomenon among very smart men. They can run conglomerates; they can win complicated cases in court; they can invent the microprocessor; they can run the country; but they can't find the butter.

Every woman I've talked to who has a man like that in her life tells me the same thing. "He's a brilliant engineer," they say, "but when I'm out of town on business, he can't figure out how to turn the dishwasher on."

So for women of all ages everywhere, I'd like to perform a public service and provide an instruction manual for men so they can change the toilet paper roll, bake a potato, do the laundry, empty the dishwasher and make dinner for themselves or any small child who is hungry.

Chapter 1

BREAKFAST WAS NOT INVENTED BY STARBUCKS

HOW TO FIND THE BUTTER

I'm starting off with finding the butter because if I start with instructions on making the toast, the toast will be cold by the time you figure out where the butter is.

I would have thought Dustin Hoffman in "Rain Man" could have figured out where the butter is, until I married you and on our first morning as man and wife, after our honeymoon at a resort in Hawaii where the butter was in little round sculpted balls right in front of you on a very small table, you came into the kitchen and kissed me and sat down at the table and said, "Where's the butter?"

I was too much in love with you to say, "Where the #$$%^% do you think the butter is? It's where the butter has always been since someone invented the butter churn. IN THE FRIDGE!"

Over the years, I waited for you to find the butter all by yourself, but since you never did, I'm leaving you instructions on finding it in case I die suddenly from an apoplectic fit.

- **First, find the kitchen.**

It's the room with the sink in it. If there's also a toilet in there, you'll know you've wandered into the powder room. Find a room with a sink and a stove in it.

- **Second, locate the refrigerator.**

It's a large white box-shaped appliance with a door.

- **Third, open the fridge and find the small door with the butter inside. It's on the right hand corner of the refrigerator door.**

Lift up this little door—you cannot slide it open.

Inside the little door you will see a glass container with something yellow inside it. That's the butter.

Take it out, lift off the glass cover, and voila! You have found the butter!

Now all you have to do is make the toast.

HOW TO MAKE TOAST

All of this is just the beginning step in making breakfast for yourself if I should desert you by going to the hospital to have my appendix out or if I should run off with the man down the street who has a house on the ocean on Cape Cod. Once you have found the butter, the next logical thing is making the toast and coffee and frying an egg without calling me in the hospital or on Cape Cod.

Let's start with the toaster. I know you've seen me make toast a thousand times, but I feel I need to be more specific about the way it works because one time I put the bread in the toaster and went off to put a load of wash in the washing machine for a couple of minutes and when I came back the bread was the same color it was when I left.

"Where's my toast?" you asked. "You poured my coffee but you didn't give me my toast." I always try to be pleasant in the morning, working on the theory that if I start off the day without saying, "You're an idiot!" I've come a long way on the evolutionary ladder and I've also taken one giant step for womankind in its vain attempt to civilize the men who stumble across their path. So I merely said, "Are you crippled? You have to get up from your chair and push the thing down to make toast."

The Anatomy of a Toaster

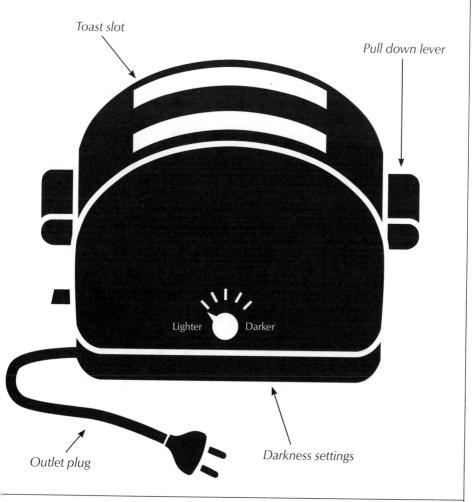

Toast slot

Pull down lever

Lighter *Darker*

Outlet plug

Darkness settings

You probably won't want the whole wheat bread because it's healthy. The rye bread says real Jewish rye but you're allowed to eat it even though we're not Jewish. Don't be confused by the "cocktail" in front of the pumpernickel. You don't have to mix a drink to eat it. But you don't want it for breakfast. Stick with the white bread.

• Decide whether you want one slice or two.

Usually it's one for breakfast and two for a sandwich. Luckily, you will remember there are two slots in the toaster in case it's lunchtime. Put the bread in the toaster. If you're only toasting one piece, it's all right. The toaster can make just one slice.

• Put the dial thing on the middle setting.

Now this part is somewhat difficult. On the front of the toaster (one of the short sides) you will see a little dial that determines how brown the toast will be. The left side of the dial is practically raw toast. The right side of the dial is burnt toast. You want something in between, so turn the dial to the middle.

• Push the lever down.

If nothing happens after a few minutes, take the plug that is attached to the toaster (there's only one plug) and put it into the electric outlet right next to the toaster. I know there are two outlets, but they both work.

• Wait for the popping noise.

That doesn't mean you've broken the toaster. It means the toast is ready.

• Butter the toast.

Put the toast on a plate (from the cupboard just above the toaster and breadbox—I planned it that way) and if you haven't lost the butter or given it away to the cleaning lady, spread some on the toast with a knife. I'm too exhausted to tell you where the knives are so see if you can figure it out yourself or eat dry toast or buy a bagel on the way to the office or go hungry. I'm losing the will to live. But I won't run away from home before I tell you how to make coffee. You'll need lots of coffee, especially if your next wife is not the saint I am.

HOW TO MAKE COFFEE

On the counter next to the breadbox there is a coffee maker. You can identify it by the glass container with a lid that sits on the bottom of the appliance. Above that glass container (which will be filled with coffee if you follow these instructions correctly) there is a black, cone-shaped part which slides open.

• Put the filter in the coffeemaker.

Slide open the black part and you will see a v-shaped opening. It's v-shaped because it was made to hold a wedge-shaped filter. Don't panic—I'll tell you exactly how to find that wedge-shaped filter.

In the drawer directly under the coffee-maker, you will see a neat pile of white, wedge-shaped filters. Take one out of the drawer and close the drawer. Very good!

Open the filter and place it into the black, cone-shaped part of the coffee maker. Press it down all around so it sticks to the black part and stays open.

• Find the coffee.

Again, I know this is confusing, but just trust me when I say go back to the refrigerator (remember?) and on the top shelf of the refrigerator (not the door of the refrigerator which also has shelves) you will see a bag of coffee. It says coffee on it, but if you're not sure, open it and smell it. Nothing smells like coffee but coffee.

Bring the coffee over to the coffee maker. If your cell rings, don't answer it because this is the most important part of the whole process.

• Put the coffee into the coffee maker.

There is a small scoop inside the bag of coffee. Scoop out four heaping scoopfuls of coffee and put them one at a time into the white coffee filter. If some of it spills on the counter, don't worry about it. You can brush the spilled coffee into the garbage bag which is under the sink. Don't confuse the garbage bag with the recycling bag which is full of... Oh, never mind, just leave the coffee on the counter—I'll fix it when I get home.

• Add water.

Now, you're almost there. Close the filter container and put your hand on the very top of the coffee maker. Lift the top up. Yes, it does too open. You will see a large hole. Fill the glass measuring cup that is always next to the coffee maker unless you moved it, with three cups of water. That's two cups and then one cup because the cup only holds two cups. Pour the water carefully into the hole in the top of the coffee maker.

• Turn the coffee maker on.

Close the lid on the top and push the small button on the base of the coffee maker to "On". If you've done it right, a red light will go on and the coffee maker will start making rude noises that sounds like someone belching. You'll like that part. In a very short time (two minutes or so) you'll have coffee. Congratulations.

Oh wait—the coffee mugs. They are in the cupboard next to the cupboard where the plates are kept. Your mug—the one with Derek Jeeter's picture on it—is in the front row.

The Anatomy of a Coffee Maker

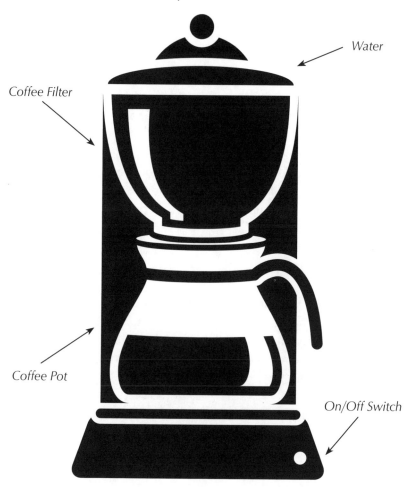

Water

Coffee Filter

Coffee Pot

On/Off Switch

HOW TO FRY AN EGG

- **Find the eggs.**

Now that you know where the refrigerator is, you won't have any trouble finding the eggs. What do you mean you looked on every shelf and there are no eggs there? Oh right. I forgot to tell you that I keep some food on the DOOR of the refrigerator. Look on the top shelf of the door and miraculoso! you will see 12 little round dents in the shelf that are filled with eggs. Take one out very carefully and try not to drop it on the floor because it would take me several pages to tell you how to clean it up. Eggs are very gloppy when they spill on the floor or... anywhere.

- **Find the frying pan.**

Don't panic. It's in a cupboard underneath the counter that has the blue bread box and the black coffeemaker and the toaster on it. Open the cupboard door, bend down and you will see several frying pans on the top shelf of the lower cupboard. Take the top one because that's the smallest.

- **Put the frying pan on one of the burners on the stove.**

There are four burners and it doesn't matter which one you use, but it's probably easiest to use the lower right hand one because then you can find the knob to turn on the gas which is directly below the burner. Turn the knob to the right and you will hear a clicking noise. It's o.k. You have not broken the stove. Turn the knob further to the right and the flame will leap up. Turn it until the flame is a nice medium height.

- **Find the butter again.**

It's wherever you put it after you made the toast. I'm sure you didn't put it back in the refrigerator because it's against your nature to put anything back where it belongs ever, so look on one of the counters. Got it? Very good. Now put a small piece of butter in the frying pan and wait until it sizzles.

- **Crack open an egg into the pan.**

Uh-oh - Not to worry, you can clean up the egg on the burner later. Put the pan on another burner and try again. Eventually you'll get the egg into the pan.

- **Pour some water into the pan and cover it with a lid.**

Not too much water and not too long. In about 24 seconds your egg will be done, and if you did it right it will look like this: If you didn't—oh well, at least you have toast and coffee.

Chapter 2

HOUSEWORK IS NOT A GENE INHERITED BY WOMEN

Can we start out with a basic premise: Housework is not nuclear physics. It doesn't compare with brain surgery even if you're cooking brains for dinner.

Nobody taught me anything about keeping house or cooking or finding a good plumber or loading a dishwasher when I was growing up. I showed no interest in any of those things and my mother just did it all herself. I do remember her grumbling about the little girl next door who refilled the ice-cube trays without having to be told and my goody-goody cousin who could shorten her own clothes and knit bed socks for our grandmother every Christmas.

I didn't care. And I have never learned to care about any of that stuff. I loved having children and playing with them and teaching them to be good people and to have lots of fun and to earn their own living so they would never have to depend on a man for money, but I only did the essential housework that I needed to do to convince people I was a fit wife and mother.

So if I could learn to find the butter, vacuum the rugs, shop in the supermarket with two small children, feed those same little children millions of times before they grew up and went off to college, and understand that you have to take the dishes out of the dishwasher and put them where they belong (in the same places 365 days a year) before you can put the dirty dishes in, then a man who went to Harvard Law School should be able to do it too. Here are the basics:

HOW TO EMPTY THE DISHWASHER AND FILL IT AGAIN

All those clean dishes in the dishwasher have to be put where they belong. Yes you can. They all go on shelves in cupboards or in drawers and you will get used to where they all go as I take more and more business trips and longer and longer vacations. I have drawn a diagram showing what goes in which drawers and cupboards, though they've been in the same places for the last twenty-seven years.

When there are no more dishes, pots, glasses or silverware in the dishwasher, you are ready to put the dirty dishes in there. I know you didn't go to Harvard to scrub frying pans and scrape icky plates, but I went to Wellesley and only part of my brain has been destroyed by doing household chores. Pay attention.

• Loading the dishwasher.

Stand the glasses up on the top shelf except for your wine glass which you place on its side wherever it fits. Small bowls and long knives go on this shelf too.

You will notice there are handy little slots on the bottom shelf where you will put the scraped plates standing up.

Next to the slots there is a flat place where you put the frying pan face down. You should have scrubbed all the nasty bits off before you put it into the dishwasher or it will come out with the nasty bits still on it.

• Put the soap in the door.

If there are no more dishes or glasses or forks anywhere in the kitchen (look under the table too) you are ready to put in the soap tab. Oh stop whining. The tabs are in a box under the sink that says "dishwasher tabs" and you take one out, take off its cellophane wrap and place it in the little place in the inside of the door of the dishwasher that has a door on it. Close the door.

• Turn the thing on.

On the outside of the door there are lots of things to push. You only have to push "Normal wash" and "Start". A nice gentle noise tells you the dishwasher has obeyed your orders and in about an hour the dishes will be washed and clean. Then you get to take them out and start all over again. And again. And again. And again.

Common Items Used To Clean Dishes

Sponge   *Brush*   *Steel Wool*

Dishwasher

HOW TO DO THE LAUNDRY

Once you have mastered the art of making dirty dishes sparkling clean, you will want to do the same thing for your dirty clothes. People do notice if you wear the same shirt for a week and they will not be polite about it. Your grandchildren will no longer come to visit and your grown children will organize an intervention, so pay attention. It's not that hard.

• Find the hamper full of dirty clothes.

It's that wicker thing in our bedroom full of towels, golf socks and things I can never identify but wash anyway. Just take a deep breath and you'll find it.

• Sort the clothes.

Why? Because if you don't, you will have gray underwear and sports shirts. I know you don't care, but I have to go out in public with you when I get home from visiting my mother, who does all the laundry perfectly and even likes to do it—I'm pretty sure she's my mother.

Put all the white clothes in one pile and all the colored things in another pile. Then divide each of those piles into underwear and sheets which go into the hot-water wash, and sports shirts and silky things which go into the cold-water wash. Otherwise you will have shrunken sports shirts and I will have wizened lingerie. Stop whining.

- **Actually put one of the piles of dirty clothes in the washer and turn it on.**

Pick up the pile of underwear and sheets. Take them into the room with the washer and dryer. Turn the dial on the left to "Large." Turn the dial in the middle to "Hot and warm". Turn the large dial to "Heavy" and pull it toward you. Not too hard or the dial will come off in your hand.

- **Put the detergent into the washer.**

Look down. See that large bottle on the floor? Dump about a capful of the blue liquid inside it into the washing machine. Throw in the underwear and sheets and go downstairs and read the sports page for half an hour.

- **Put the clean, washed, wet clothes into the dryer.**

Go back upstairs and if no noise is coming from the washer and the dial is on "Off", you're ready to put the clothes into the dryer. I'm trusting you to know that's the other appliance in that room. Throw the clothes in there, and set the dryer on "High and "Heavy." The clothes should be dry in an hour. But don't leave yet.

• Wash the rest of the clothes.

After you have taken the clothes out of the dryer and thrown them on a chair for me to deal with when I get back home, go back to the bedroom and pick up the sports shirts and lingerie pile and bring them into the room with the washer.

Keep the left hand dial on "Large". Put the middle dial on "Cold" and set the large dial on "Permanent press" and pull it toward you. The water should start running into the washer.

Repeat what you did before and you're finished for about an hour and a half. And I've never loved you more.

Darks and lights should be separated

Common Items Used To Clean Clothes

Stain remover

Laundry detergent

Washer

Dryer

HOW TO CLEAN THE BATHROOM

A dirty bathroom is a sign of a bad person. If you can't clean the disgusting things that lurk in a bathroom, then you're not fit to be a part of the American way of life. I had to learn this lesson the hard way when I shared an apartment with three other women in New York before I was married, and found out that we had to take turns cleaning the bathroom.

Since I had managed to avoid this whole sordid thing by having a mother and then a community bathroom in college, I didn't take kindly to this particular way of spending every third Saturday morning. In fact, I tried to get away with mopping out the sink with a couple of Kleenexes as my contribution to the cleanliness-is-next-to-godliness ethic in that apartment.

Unfortunately, I roomed with two other women whose mothers forced them to learn how to maintain a sparkling, germ-free, practically sterile bathroom, so I had to learn too. I'm passing along to you the least distasteful ways to clean the bathroom, I'll come home some day and take over for you before you degenerate into an outcast from society, scorned by good people everywhere. We'll start with the shower:

The tiles get grungy and sad looking if you don't clean them with this stuff especially made for cleaning tiles. Don't tell me you can't find it. It's under the sink. In that cabinet under the sink. LOOK FOR IT. Sorry, didn't mean to lose my temper, but sometimes... okay. The tile cleaner is in a bucket under the sink with a sponge.

No, you can't just spray on the cleaner and let it ooze down the wall to the drain. Because you just can't. Start at the top and spray it on. Then wipe with a wet sponge—I don't know why it has to be wet, it just does. Be sure to scrub the white grouting in between the tiles.

It does matter because if we ever decide to sell this house, the first thing a prospective buyer looks at is the tile in the bathrooms. If the grouting is dingy and uncared for and miserable, the buyer will try to hide his look of disgust and say under his breath to the realtor, "I could never live in this house. The grouting is disgusting." Laugh if you want to, but check this with any real estate agent and you'll see that I'm right. And if I come home to a lovely, clean shower, I'll take one with you.

If you've been leaving gobs of toothpaste in the sink while I'm away, then it will have hardened and you'll have to scrub it with a sponge and Ajax to get the gunk up. Serves you right.

Clean the sink and the counter around it and polish up the faucets with the stuff in the green bottle. Oh, I don't know why you use a window cleaner on chrome faucets. You just do! Trust me. Some things don't have an answer. (Why don't we have a cleaning woman is another question I'd like answered, for instance.)

And while you have that glass cleaner out, spray the mirrors and sponge them off until there are no streaks or flossing splotches on them and you can see your frowning face clearly.

Now this next part is gross, but I can't help it, you have to do it or guests will never come to our house again. (That is not a good thing.) The toilet.

Since you were well trained by your mother, who raised three sons, to put the toilet seat back down again after you have peed, you may not be aware that the underside of the toilet seat has to be sprayed with stuff in that other bottle under the sink and scrubbed with another sponge. It's not that bad!

Then a quick mopping of the top of the toilet seat and the lid and the rest of the outside of the toilet and you're ready to swish out the inside of the toilet with that little mop standing next to it. Courage. You only have the floor to wash.

But before you attack the floor, there's something very important I wish you'd learn to do.
It's something I've tried to teach you over the years, but you don't

seem to understand how to do it. It's really so simple.

It must be a guy thing that you can't learn it because all my friends have the same problem. And they're all married to really smart guys like you too.

What is it about you geniuses that you can't put a new roll of toilet paper on the metal holder after you use up the last roll of toilet paper?

The funniest "Mad About You" I ever saw was the one where Helen Hunt came into the living room with a roll of toilet paper and that metal holder and inserted the cardboard roll of the toilet paper over the metal holder. She didn't say a word about the toilet paper. She was yelling at Paul about something else and while she yelled, she did the toilet paper mime. The whole audience roared with laughter, and I knew she had hit a chord. It wasn't just me and my friends. It was women and men everywhere.

See, my theory is that it's one of those things your mother always did so it never occurred to you that it's one of those things ANYBODY CAN DO, EVEN MEN.

So one more time here, buddy. I know you can do it.

Reach in the cabinet under the sink and grab a roll of toilet paper.

Then pull the metal rod with the empty cardboard roll on it out of its holder, throw the cardboard roll away and slide the new roll of toilet paper onto the metal rod and put it back in its holder. See how easy that was. What do you mean the metal roll fell apart and a spring jumped out and rolled in back of the toilet? Oh never mind. I'll do it when I get home.

The bathroom is small, so you can do the floor in a short time. Take the sponge mop—no, it's not under the sink, it's in the basement with the rest of the cleaning stuff—and put some water and a squirt of Fantastic in the bucket, and mop up the floor. Put everything away—don't just leave it there—I won't be home until Thursday—and go downstairs and open a beer.

I usually drink a half bottle of wine when I finish the bathroom, but you need to be alert and ready to start your next chore: vacuuming. Compared to the bathroom, this will seem like a vacation.

Common Items in the Bathroom

Toilet

Sink

Bathtub

HOW TO VACUUM

I know that before you even start reading this part of your instruction manual, you're all red in the face yelling, "I wouldn't have to vacuum if you hadn't insisted on white wall-to-wall carpeting in the living room and dining room and light blue rugs in the bedroom and beige carpeting going up the stairs."

But even if we had left the marked-up, scratched, hideous wood floors that were here when we bought the house, you'd still have to vacuum because the tracked-in dirt would show up even more on wood than on rugs. So go find the vacuum.

I've left notes and arrows leading to the vacuum cleaner in the hall closet. I understand that putting all the parts together is going to be a challenge, but please don't call me when I'm in the middle of a conference because all the other women there will start giggling and we'll never get anything done.

Do you see the little cord with the small plug on the end of it? That does not go into the wall, so don't even try. It goes up into a hole next to the handle, where there is a tiny outlet and I'm really grateful I won't be there to hear you cursing and swearing while you try to fit the tiny plug into the tiny outlet without being able to see it. You just have to keep turning the plug until it fits in.

I know you like to know ahead of time exactly how to do something before you do it—I remember you once read a book on how to ride a horse before you went to a dude ranch out west—but this is one of those things you just have to fool around with until it works.

Once you have joined the two parts of the vacuum together, find the large plug that does go into the wall on the canister. The canister is what they call the main part of the vacuum cleaner. When you have plugged it into the wall, you're ready to roll.

You might want to plug yourself into your ipod while you're at it because a little jazz never hurts when you're doing something boring. Just vacuum the main parts of the rugs, and the wooden floor in the kitchen and the tile floor in the bathroom. Oops, should have told you to do this before you washed the bathroom floor, but never mind, do it anyway. It can't hurt.

If you find the vacuum isn't sucking up the way it should—and I have great sympathy for it when it doesn't—it's probably because you need to change the vacuum cleaner bag. In fact, you should really check this before you start vacuuming because I don't think I changed the bag after I cleaned up the Christmas tree needles in the living room. Yes I know it's March. Oh, shut up and change the damn bag.

In order to do this, you have to open up the canister part (the bottom part) and you will see a full bag attached to a round hole. Notice exactly how that bag is attached to that round hole, so you can put the new one on the same way. Take the old one out, don't drop it or you'll have a lot more vacuuming to do than you planned on, throw it out, put the new one on, close the canister and you're ready to... What's that? You can't find the vacuum cleaner bags.

Oh sorry. I meant to tell you that they're either in the closet in the hall where you found the vacuum—that's where they're supposed to be—or if I didn't put them in the closet after I bought them, they could be with the other cleaning supplies in the basement—or I might have left them in the bag I put my groceries in now that I have to supply my own bag and don't have paper bags to throw out anymore because of the environment, or I might have forgotten to buy them altogether. Oh just use the old bag and do the best you can. That's all any of us can do after all.

When you have finished vacuuming, please don't leave the vacuum cleaner in the middle of the living room floor, thinking that I will come home again some day and will know what to do with it. It's true. I do know where it goes. I'm the one who decided where to put the vacuum cleaner when we were married, and I know how to put it in that hall closet where you found it.

But I won't be back for three more days and if you don't put it away, the cat will never come out from under the bed to go to the litter box or eat her food or drink her water because she's scared to death of the noise the vacuum cleaner makes and hides until it is no longer in sight.

HOW TO DO THE IRONING

Since the American Psychological Association's annual convention is in Hawaii this year, I will be away for a whole week.

But I know you'll be just fine here. When you get hungry, just call the pizza place and when you get bored, watch a baseball game. If you run out of clean clothes, read the part of this manual on doing laundry.

There's only one thing I'm worried about though. If you do the laundry and you take a wrinkled shirt out of the dryer, will you know how to iron it? Don't say you'll just wait until I get home because what if I like Hawaii so much I decide to stay there, or what if my plane is hijacked, or what if I get amnesia?

So, here are some simple instructions for ironing your shirt:

- **First look in that closet where you found the vacuum cleaner—what? You didn't vacuum yet? Well, you can do that after you iron. Inside you will find the ironing board.**

Set it up anywhere. In front of the TV is probably a good place. The iron is somewhere in that closet. You must have seen an iron before. Your mother was always ironing when I came over. Anyway, look for something that looks like the picture to the right:

Ironing board   *Iron*

- **Next, pour some water in that little hole in the top of the iron and set the dial on cotton and steam. When the iron is hot—what do you mean, how will you know? When you burn your finger testing it, of course.**

Okay, spread the shirt out on the ironing board and run the iron over the whole shirt. If the phone rings, don't put the iron down on the shirt and leave it there while you go to answer the phone, because you will have a large black iron shaped mark on your shirt when you get off the phone. It's not attractive.

So once the shirt is wrinkle-free and sweet-smelling (if you put Bounce in the dryer) you can wear it to meet me at the airport (I decided to come home after all). I love you.

Chapter 3

PREGNANT WIVES AND THE BABY THAT COMES AFTERWARD

HOW TO TREAT A PREGNANT WIFE WITHOUT COMPLAINING ABOUT ANYTHING WHILE MAKING HER FEEL SEXY AND DESIRABLE AT ALL TIMES

Your wife has just told you that you are about to become a father for the first time. You are ecstatic, more in love with your wife than ever, eager for this new adventure to begin. In nine months you will be a father! Nine months. Easy for you to say. Not so easy for your wife. So here are some suggestions that will help you as her body changes dramatically in the coming months. Pay attention.

The first three months are the hardest until you get to the last two months. Your lively, sweet, agreeable, ready to go anywhere, do anything wife will be tired those first three months. She will not bound out of bed, making breakfast, going to work, playing with you as readily as she did before this baby started growing inside her.

Here's what not to do:

- **Whine**

- **Whimper**

- **Sigh loudly**

- **Complain or**

- **Snivel**

Instead what you want to do for this incredible woman who is carrying your baby is:

- **Bring her breakfast in bed**

- **Cook for her**

- **Do the dishes**

- **Do the laundry**

- **Vacuum and**

- **Tell her how beautiful she is and tell her you love her**

The next three months are easier. She will get her energy back, be cheerful, smile for no reason at all and SHOP.

She needs clothes with expanding waistbands and blousy tops, comfortable shoes, and especially a beautiful dress that fits over her growing belly that she can wear to parties and out to dinner and feel glamorous and unpregnant.

The last month of your wife's pregnancy is the hardest because she will be convinced the baby is never coming out and soon, you will be too. She will get bigger and bigger and BIGGER until you think she might be another octomom.

During this month, do all the things you did during the first three months only more of everything. She'll have a problem even getting out of a chair.

When she says "Do you still find me attractive?" you say, "I find you more attractive than ever, more beautiful than you've ever been in your whole life, the sexiest I've ever seen you even when we first made love, the most radiant, gorgeous, heavenly, magnificent woman—for the very reason that you are pregnant and glowing with the beauty of motherhood. I love that there is more of you to love."

Memorize those words and say them often and with heartfelt sincerity. You have to mean them.

And don't even let one tiny shred of the feeling that soon she will have the baby and be thin again and everything will be the way it was before creep into your male mind. It will be years before you can make love any time you want, on the spur of the moment, in any room of the house, wildly and loudly and hanging from the chandelier. But I'll explain all this in the next part of this chapter on learning how to go for three months without sleep.

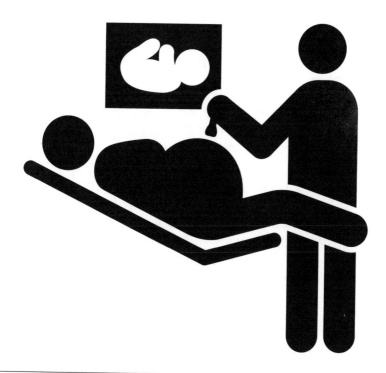

HOW TO GO WITHOUT SLEEP FOR THREE MONTHS AFTER THE BABY IS BORN

You thought the hard part was over, didn't you? The last few weeks while you and your extremely pregnant (and of course extremely attractive) wife waited for that baby to decide to be born.

Then the rush to the hospital, watching your brave, perfect wife push that little baby out into the world.

Your love for her as you watch her in labor.

And then the rush of emotion as they brought your child to you to hold. Was there ever a more beautiful baby in the world? Of course not.

Then you bring the baby home.

Of course you knew that babies cry, that they don't sleep through the night right away, that even though your wife is nursing this baby, you'll still wake up to keep her company, that you have to get up and go to work in the morning, because a lot of your friends are having first babies too and you see them falling asleep at their desks. But knowing all this and living through it without losing your job and your mind are different things.

How to Figure Out Why Your Baby Is Crying

The first thing you have to learn is to distinguish between different cries.

The Hungry Cry

You first assume it's a hungry cry and that's easy to deal with. You will get the MVP award of the year if you get up, change the baby and bring her to your wife to nurse so she gets a couple of extra minutes to wake up.

No Discernible Reason Cry

But what do you do if the baby wakes up a half hour later and cries and isn't really hungry? That's where the expression "walking the floor" originated. Someone has to get up and pick up that little baby and walk around rocking and soothing her, or sit in a rocking chair (buy one if you don't have one—they're still the best way to soothe a baby) and sing to your baby or talk to her or do anything creative that comes to mind. You will earn points for doing this that will last until at least next Wednesday with your wife.

Sometimes you can distract babies from whatever is bothering them by playing music and dancing with them. Sometimes your dog can intrigue them by coming up close and laying his head in your lap next to the baby.

Wet Diaper Crying

Sometimes babies just need a change of scene or a different position or clean diapers. And be glad you live now instead of when your mother had you. In those days, you had to use cloth diapers and safety pins and keep the smelly diapers in a large container until the diaper service came to take them away and bring you clean ones. You had to somehow hold that squirming, kicking baby down while you cleaned him off, wrapped him in a clean diaper and somehow stuck the pins in the diaper and not in the baby. Now you just whisk off the paper panties, throw them away, clean your baby off, and whisk on clean ones.

I've Got Gas Crying

And then there's that little gas bubble that didn't get patted away the last time your wife fed him which could be causing pain that makes him cry. Just put him on your shoulder and gently rub your hand over his back, pressing lightly, until you hear a hearty burp. That should do it and you can put your sleeping baby back into his bassinet until the next time. Which I hate to tell you, will be only a couple of hours away.

Fortunately this crying doesn't last until the baby is a teenager. It's really those first three months while the baby grows enough to take more food into his stomach at one feeding so that he isn't hungry so often.

But the absolute best cure for a crying baby is a grandmother. And grandmothers love babies whether they're crying, sleeping, pooping, drooling or anything else they want to do. Grandmothers are so glad to get their hands on a new baby again they will gladly go without sleep for three months without even yawning.

So if you can get your mother or your wife's mother to come over for a week or two when the baby is born and give the baby a bottle in the middle of the night so that both of you can sleep, and then come back during the day to clean the house, cook some meals, play with the baby, count your blessings and enjoy a nap.

Once those first three months are over, your baby will probably sleep through the night, smile at you whenever he sees you, and every day he will learn something new. How to roll over. How to sit up. How to crawl. How to walk. How to talk. You will be enthralled with each new thing he learns to do and you will bore everyone you know by telling them about it. That's okay. Do it anyway. You're a dad!

HOW TO WATCH FOOTBALL AND THE BABY AT THE SAME TIME

Babies sleep a lot but usually not at the time you want them to. So just when you're sure the baby is fast asleep and you can pop a Heineken and settle down on the couch to watch the game, the baby will start crying. You are not allowed to put the baby out on the porch until the game is over or turn up the volume so you can't hear him. Because.

- **First try giving the baby a bottle, burp him and put him in his little seat and place it on the couch next to you.**

The baby will look up at you with those big blue eyes and you will think he's enjoying the game too. Sorry. He only responds to cartoons not huge men crashing into each other like trucks. He will wrinkle up his little face and make an experimental whimper. Do something NOW or he will work himself up to a raging, sobbing, unstoppable noise and you will miss the first down or whatever it's called.

- **Pick up the baby at the first wail, and put him against your shoulder and gently pat his back and make soothing noises.**

Do not yell if some great lout of a player makes a brilliant play or the baby will never stop crying. Stay quiet. Rock him back and forth. Make soothing noises. Sing to him. I don't know what song! But probably not "Pants on the Ground."

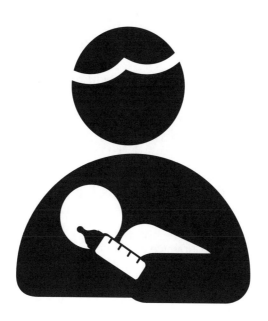

- **If this doesn't work (and it won't), stand up, still holding the baby and walk around the room gently rocking him, and don't bump into anything because you're trying to watch the game at the same time.**

If you do bump into anything and hurt some part of your body, do not swear loudly because this immediately causes more crying on the part of the baby.

- **If this doesn't work (it won't), put the baby in his carriage and wheel it around the room rocking it and moving it until he falls asleep (he won't).**

- **If the baby is still crying (he will be), take him out to the car and strap him in his car seat, turn the game on softly and drive to Ohio if necessary, until he is sleeping soundly and you can turn around and come home.**

- **Do NOT call me on my cell and say, "I can't stop this baby from crying and I'm missing the playoff! You'll have to come home."**

I will pretend that your voice is breaking up and that I can't understand a word you're saying.

Chapter 4

HOW TO TAKE CARE OF THREE
SMALL BOYS AND STAY SANE

HOW TO PUT SNOWSUITS ON THREE CHILDREN

I don't know how to break this to you, but before you can go to the supermarket to get all the stuff you'll need for feeding your children, you have to squeeze, push, pummel and bend them to get them into their snowsuits. I am in my bathing suit in Hawaii at the moment at my business conference, so you'll excuse a small smile that I am not there with you.

Oh, as I was saying, snowsuits. The two older boys can pretty much get into their jackets and pants and boots and mittens and hats by themselves, though they will get distracted when Alex takes Ian's jacket and throws it on top of the lamp and Ian will then try to kill Alex and throw his boots out into the snow. You will have to retrieve the boots, dry them off, separate the boys, threaten them with no TV forever, and tell them to get ready to go out.

However, you don't want to do this until you have wrestled Mike into his snowsuit and boots and mittens and hat because this will take you a lot longer than you think it's going to take you and if the older boys are already in their jackets and pants and boots and hats and mittens they will be overheated and cranky and no fun at all to take to the supermarket. (It's not going to be fun whether they're overheated or not, but you'll find that out for yourself when you read the next section.)

O.K, so here's how to get Mike ready and I can hear you sneering, "What could be so hard about getting Mike into a snowsuit and boots and mittens and a hat?" But what you don't realize is that he will keep moving and running away and bending over and hitting his big brothers, which will make them try to hit him, all the time you are trying to fit him into the snowsuit. You can try telling him what a big boy he is and how great he looks in his new hat and make a game out of wiggling his hands into the mittens, but your main problem will be to get him to push his feet into the boots.

You'll keep saying and then yelling, "Push!" and he'll keep saying "I am pushing" and when you try to push he'll start crying and saying, "That hurts," and you'll wonder why you didn't marry a Japanese wife who would be home doing this and not drinking margaritas in Hawaii at some trumped up psychological conference. Anyway, when you've finally got Mike's boots on and the older boys are dressed, pile them all into the car, put seat belts on everything that moves and head for the supermarket.

HOW TO SHOP IN THE SUPERMARKET
WITH THREE SMALL BOYS

When you run out of things like milk and bread and hot dogs and veggies and paper towels and cereal and lemonade, you will have to go to the supermarket or you will have three cranky little boys on your hands. Make a list and stick to it or you will have a refrigerator full of stuff I'll have to throw out when I get home.

I have printed out directions to the supermarket. If you get lost, one of the boys can tell you how to get there, and yes, you do have to take all three boys with you. I know Alex is eight, but that's too young to babysit his brothers.

At the supermarket, get a cart, put Mike in the seat of the cart, lift Ian into the cart, and threaten Alex with a frozen dinner if he gets more than two feet away from you.

You will notice that the supermarket aisles have large signs over each one telling you what is in that aisle. That doesn't help you if you are looking for capers or bread crumbs, but it's a start. At one end of the supermarket they keep all the vegetables and fruits. At the other end they have all the meat and chicken. In the back of the market is a fish counter. One aisle has all the butter, eggs, milk, cheese, and that most important food group—ice cream.

If you can't find something, ask Alex because he knows where everything is. He will ask you to buy any gourmet item he sees (like venison, pheasant, or quail in the meat department or crème fraiche in dairy) but you must say no and mean it. Even if you want some, you won't know how to cook it.

Go up and down each aisle until you have found everything on your list and some things you forgot to put on the list. If Ian complains that there are too many things on top of him in the basket, tell him you're sorry and you're almost through. That usually works.

If Mike says he has to go to the bathroom, just say, "No, you don't." That sometimes works and sometimes doesn't. Make sure Alex is with you at all times. He has a way of disappearing when you're reaching for something on a top shelf and unless you want his picture to turn up on a milk carton, yell his name in an "I-mean-it" voice until he appears again.

When you think you have everything you need (there's always something you needed badly but forgot to buy so you'll have to go back again the next day), find a check-out counter with the least amount of customers waiting in line.

Put all your stuff on the counter—I think of it as a form of exercise (bend and stretch), since I hardly have time to go to the gym anymore—and count to make sure you have all the children still with you. Make sure Ian is still breathing and that Mike hasn't wet his pants yet and that Alex is the child standing next to you.

Hand the cashier your supermarket card (I put it in your wallet) so you will get any discounts they are offering that day.

When the cashier tells you the astronomical amount of money you owe for a couple of days supply of food and paper products, give her cash or a check or put your credit card through the little machine they have there at the counter.

Put all the bags in the cart next to and around Ian, make sure Alex is still with you, and tell Mike what a good boy he is to wait until he gets home to go to the bathroom. That'll buy you a few more minutes.

Wheel the cart to the parking lot. Take out all the bags and put them in the back of the car. Check to make sure that the three boys with you are yours and then put them in the car and tell them to fasten their seat belts.

Drive home, unload the car, send Mike immediately to the bathroom, put the food away (I don't care—put it anywhere. I'll fix it when I get home or out of the hospital), and rejoice—you don't have to do it again for two whole days.

HOW TO MAKE DINNER FOR THE CHILDREN

Before you start, let me tell you a little about your children: Alex will only eat food that tastes like it has been prepared by a gourmet chef. Don't worry though, the pediatrician has assured me that he will eat when he is really hungry and will not starve to death if you cook dinner.

Ian eats everything you put in front of him and says thank you when you serve him. Be very grateful for this child.

Michael will only eat white foods, so I have left you filet of sole to make for this dinner. He will eat the inside of a baked potato, but don't even try making him a vegetable because they are all colored green or orange or yellow.

Ready. Here you go:

- **An hour before you want to eat, turn on the oven.**

Yes you can. On the front of the stove—think of it as a dashboard— you will see the word "bake". Touch that word with your finger. It's like a computer without the mouse. Instantly the number in the middle of the dashboard will show 350 degrees. That's good. Touch "bake" again and the oven will start heating up. It is a very obliging oven and will beep when it has reached the desired temperature. This takes about 6 minutes.

- **While you are waiting for the oven to beep, find the potatoes.**

They have their own special drawer, just to the right of the stove. Open the lower drawer and you will see lots of potatoes there. If you see pot holders and dish cloths, you have opened the wrong drawer. Take out four medium-sized potatoes. If you can't figure out what a medium sized potato is, it doesn't matter. Just take out four potatoes and wash them. Yes, you do have to wash them.

- **When the stove beeps at you, put the washed and dried potatoes in the oven on the top shelf.**

They take an hour to cook, so you can make sure the children aren't killing each other before you come back to make the fish and the vegetables (for Alex and Ian).

- **Open the refrigerator.**

(That's the appliance that has the magnet on it with a picture of a cat and it says, "Husband and cat missing. $25 reward for return of the cat." It's just a joke—don't be offended). I put the fish on the top shelf and cleared away everything else on that shelf, so you will be able to identify it easily.

Take out the fish, the butter (remember it's on the top shelf of the refrigerator door if you put it back after breakfast. If you didn't, good luck), and the asparagus (in the large drawer on the bottom shelf of the fridge).

• Find the frying pan.

In case you forgot where the frying pans are, they are in the cupboard under the counter that has the toaster on it. Stoop down and take out a large frying pan. It doesn't matter which one.

• Put a lot of butter in the pan.

About half a stick of butter. Throw the fish in the butter when it sizzles and cook the four filets about 3 minutes to a side. Use a spatula (a big flat thing with a handle) which is in the drawer next to the drawer with the knives and forks. I know there are a lot of other strange things in that drawer too, but the spatula is the only thing that looks like it could turn a fish over.

• Get the asparagus ready to cook.

Cut off the tough ends (about two inches), wrap it in a paper towel, sprinkle some water on the paper towel and put it in the microwave (next to the toaster). Push 5.00 on the front of the microwave and hit "start". The glass plate in there will begin to turn slowly if you have done this correctly.

• Call one of the children.

Probably Ian because he complains the least about everything. It has something to do with his being a middle child. Anyway, ask him to put forks and napkins on the table and ask him to pour three glasses of milk (he knows where it is). You can pour your own large glass of wine when you're ready.

Take four plates from the plate cupboard. Put them out on the counter.

Take a long-handled fork (in the spatula drawer) and spear each of the potatoes and put one on each plate.

Excellent. Go back to the dashboard and push "cancel" so the oven will turn off.

Take your spatula and scoop up each filet and put one on each plate.

If one side is burned, put the unburned side up. Only Alex will complain and you can tell him you cooked the fish "Cajun style". I do that all the time, and sometimes it works.

Open the microwave door, take out the asparagus, throw out the wet paper towel and put a few stalks of asparagus on three of the plates (Mike won't eat any because they're green).

• Open the potatoes with a fork.

Put some sour cream on them (it's in the fridge in a small carton labeled "sour cream"—you can't miss it—well you could miss it, in which case use butter because you know where that is—right?) in the middle of each one. If you sprinkle some chives on Alex's, he will be ecstatic.

•Throw some more butter on the asparagus, and you're ready to eat.

You can turn the ball game on while they're eating if you want because it distracts them from the meal and they won't care what they're eating. I know this is against all the rules of proper child rais-ing, but I'm trying to help you out here.

After you have all eaten your dinner, you will have to put the dirty dishes in the dishwasher, so see above for instructions.

Now that wasn't so bad, was it? Honey?

Food Suitable for Dinner

Hot Dogs   Steak   Pasta

Food **NOT** Suitable for Dinner

Cake   Candy   Ice Cream

HOW TO BATHE THREE LITTLE BOYS

You're almost through! Just one more fun-filled event and you're ready to collapse in front of the TV and appreciate what a wonderful wife you have who does all these things every day, every week, every month, for years and years and never complains, always smiling, a joy and a blessing to come home to each night, secure in the knowledge that she has made a pact with the devil which will allow her to win a Pulitzer, an academy award, or the presidency of the United States, once she has completed this part of her life, raising three fine boys.

Are you ready for bath time and three slippery little boys who are badly in need of a bath but determined to make it as difficult for you as possible to get them into the tub, dry them all off before they drip all over our bed and the dog, keep them from getting dirty again before you get them into clean pajamas and at last! into bed?

The secret of doing this—especially of doing this without getting soaking wet yourself—is to:

- **Wear something that had to go in the wash anyway.**

- **Bribe your three sons with ice cream and a story if they cooperate.**

- **Tell yourself that your wife will be home tomorrow and you can go back to reading or watching tv or drinking heavily when she gets back.**

Fill the bathtub with warm water and bubble bath before the boys undress, then throw all the toys you can find into the water—not the water guns, however, or you will have to wipe up the whole bathroom, including the ceiling, after the bath. There's one really neat motor boat that winds up and zooms through the water. Don't let the older boys aim it at Mike.

Keep a tight grip on Mike so the other two boys won't drown him. Distract them by getting them to make soap bubble figures out of the bubble bath. Oh use your imagination. You can do Santa Claus or poodles or rabbits or dinosaurs or—oh, just figure it out.

For the five seconds this will get them to hold still, wash their faces, especially their ears and behind their ears, their necks and as much of their upper bodies as you can manage before they get bored with the soap bubble figures and try to drown Mike again. Don't worry about the bottom halves of your children, because they are immersed in soap suds that will do the job. And I'll do the shampoos when I get home. You'll never manage that.

About drying them. Each child has his own towel with his name on it, and each one is a different color. Be sure you give them the right towel or one or all three towels will end up the bathtub. Wrap Mike up in his towel and sit on the toilet seat (lid down) and dry him. That's the fun part because he's such a cuddly little boy.

Supervise the other two boys as they dry themselves and once again, make sure they don't injure each other severely. It can happen from some innocent remark by Alex to Ian such as, "You're stupid!" followed by Ian's outraged "You're stupid!" and an attempt to bash each other's head against the tile walls. Threaten them with no ice cream. That usually works.

When all three boys are dry and in their pajamas, they will look so clean and adorable you'll be tempted to relax. Do not do that. They can easily undo all your hard work in one minute's smearing of ice cream in each other's hair. Since I won't be home to shampoo their hair until tomorrow, you must separate them while they are eating the ice cream and maybe turn on TV and let them watch a Seinfeld re-run. Stay alert, even though you are laughing at Jerry and his friends because the boys are just waiting for that one moment when they can eat Mike's ice cream. You do not want that to happen. If you get them successfully through the ice cream obstacle, persuade them to brush their teeth and get into bed for a story. Good luck finding one book they all want to hear that particular night. Be sure and read the whole book because they will notice if you leave out a page or two.

Kiss them good night, and try not to think about tomorrow morning when you will get all three boys ready for pre-school and school. And remember, I love you.

Chapter 5

IF YOU CAN RUN A CONGLOMERATE, YOU CAN ANSWER THE DAMN PHONE

HOW TO ANSWER A RINGING TELEPHONE

A recent study of 1,000 men and 1,000 women showed that men can sit within one foot of a telephone ringing ten times or until the voice mail picks up and never reach over to answer the phone.

Women, on the other hand, pick up the phone on the first "Ri..."

Scientists discovered that there is a shut-off valve in men's brains that turns off the sounds of a ringing phone, a crying baby, a talking wife and a whining mother. This explains why a man can totally ignore the phone.

The first step in re-training this part of his brain to open the shut-off valve is to explain why he should answer it. Here are a few reasons he might understand:

- **It could be your wife calling from the emergency room saying she has been hit by a bus.**

- **It could be a teenage daughter stranded at the mall.**

- **It could be your mother saying she misses the sound of your voice.**

Different Types of Telephones

- **It could be somebody from Nigeria telling you he has been emailing you to tell you you have won ten million dollars if you wouldn't mind sending $4,362 to him in the next mail.**

Leave a post-it stuck to his beer-drinking hand with specific instructions for the next time the phone rings:

Identify the ringing noise. Mute the sound on the TV remote and if the ringing continues, it's the phone next to your chair.

Don't assume someone will pick it up. There's nobody home, your secretary is in the office, and your mother is home crying because you never call her.

Say, "Hello," or "Tom here," or "Yes?" but say something so the other person on the other end will know you're there.

Here's how to deal with almost any possible caller:

If it's a telemarketer, tell him you'll call him back when he's eating dinner and ask for his phone number.

If it's one of the children's friends, tell them to call your child on his cell and never to call the house again.

If it's your wife, say "I'm so glad you called. I have been waiting to talk to you all day. You're the only woman I will ever love."

If it's one of your children say, "No you can't have any more money," or "No, you can't stay out until 3 in the morning," or "No, your mother won't pick you up either."

If it's an obscene phone caller, say, "My phone is on a permanent tap by the FBI because I'm an assistant U.S. Attorney and they use it to catch criminals who call and threaten me."

If it's your mother, say, "Hi, Mom. I was just going to call you and tell you I love you."

At the end of the conversation, say, "Thanks for calling"(except for the telemarketer or the obscene caller) and put the top of the phone back on the bottom part. If you hear strange sounds coming out of the phone and a voice saying, "Please hang up and try your call again," you've hung the phone up upside down.

Realize what a rewarding experience answering the phone can be and resolve to try it again even when your wife is home.

Scientists expect that with proper conditioning by wives and girl-friends, the shut-off valve in the male brain will become a vestigial organ and be totally useless.

HOW TO PACK A SUITCASE
FOR A BUSINESS TRIP

I know you've done this a thousand times by yourself, but there are a couple of things I thought I ought to mention since I'm not there at the moment to talk you down.

• **Did you remember to wash your underwear?**

You may remember—probably not—that as I said goodbye to you at the airport on my way to my business conference, I kissed you and said, "Honey, don't forget to do a load of laundry before you leave for New York next week or you won't have any clean underwear and socks." Your mind was already back at the house where the game was about to start so I'm sure you didn't hear a word I said, even though you said, "Sure, honey, sure. Have a safe trip."

• **If you were listening and you did do a load of wash (see instructions under Housework) and you do have clean underwear, there's no problem.**

• **If you weren't listening and you didn't do a load of laundry and you have to leave in fifteen minutes, I can't help you.**

Just wear the same underwear for four days and convince yourself you smell rugged. Or pay the exorbitant rate the hotel charges and have them wash your clothes.

- **I meant to tell you that when I picked up your dress shirts from the cleaners, they didn't fold them and put them in boxes. They put them on hangers, so you're going to have to fold them yourself.**

Don't yell. Here's a step by step illustration of how to fold a shirt.

Step #1
Lay shirt out flat.

Step #2
Fold one sleeve over.

Step #3
Fold the other sleeve over.

Step #5
Fold bottom of shirt to the top.

Step #5
Flip the shirt over and you're done.

- Last time I was away, you packed your razor without the cord. Try to remember the cord so you don't have to buy another one when you get to New York like you did last time.

- I know you'll remember everything else—got your toothpaste?—and that you'll give a great presentation and no one will notice your wrinkled shirt.

Don't Forget to Pack...

Scissors for nose & ear hairs

*Comb used for hair
left on your head*

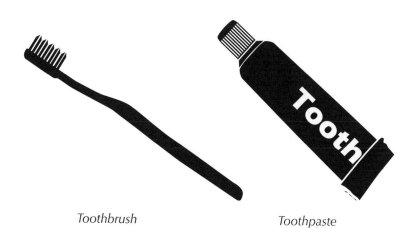

Toothbrush

Toothpaste

HOW TO FIND YOUR: WALLET, KEYS, GLASSES, SOCKS, UNDERWEAR

I don't say it anymore. I tried every way I could think of to say it in different ways. I tried holding you close and murmuring it into your ear. I tried sitting down with you for a reasonable discussion. I tried yelling it until my face turned blue. I tried ignoring the whole problem and pretending it had nothing to do with me.

But none of this worked!

So now I'm writing it down and making 100 copies of it and depositing it in your coat pocket, in your attaché case, on your computer keyboard, in your underwear drawer, under your pillow, on the seat of the car, pinned onto the back of your childrens' shirts, and on my sexiest nightgown.

IF YOU HAVE A SPECIFIC PLACE FOR YOUR POSSESSIONS AND ALWAYS PUT THEM BACK IN THAT SPECIFIC PLACE WHEN YOU ARE THROUGH WITH THEM, YOU WON'T ALWAYS LOSE THEM.

OR

PUT YOUR $%^$&^%$^%$& STUFF BACK WHERE IT BELONGS

The reason this is so important to me is that you always lose your wallet or your keys or your glasses or your socks or your underwear when you have to leave the house in five minutes and I am in the middle of getting three little boys ready for pre-school so I can get to my office on time. (My parents taught me that it is a sin against God to ever be late for anything.)

"Where are my keys?" you yell and your tone of voice implies that it is my fault that you cannot find them.

"Did you look on the hook next to the door that has a label above it saying 'Tom's keys'?" I ask in a reasonable, calm tone, while stuffing Mike into his boots, zipping up Ian's jacket and putting Alex's hat on his head.

"OF COURSE I DID AND THEY'RE NOT THERE!!" you shout, even madder at me that the keys are not where they are supposed to be.

"Why didn't you... put them back on the hook?" I start to say, but then I realize it's hopeless. It will always be hopeless. Take several deep breaths and try to remember that I married this man because I love him and for the most part he is an excellent husband and loving father. I try to call up the saintly side of me that stays calm through housewifery, motherhood, and executivedom. I hear my mother's voice in the back of my head saying, "This is the best part of your life, darling." And pulling myself together, gathering all my strength and taking another deep breath I say:

"I DON'T KNOW WHERE YOU PUT YOUR DAMN KEYS AND I DON'T GIVE A FLYING FIG WHAT YOU DID WITH THEM AND DID YOU LOOK IN YOUR RAINCOAT POCKET?"

There is a long silence while you look in your raincoat pocket and find your keys and are too embarrassed to tell me you found them.

"Did you find them?" I ask, shepherding the boys toward the garage and putting on my coat and grabbing my briefcase.

"Of course," you say. "They were right where I left them."

It wouldn't be so bad if all this weren't repeated the next day and the next and ad infinitum when you lose your wallet (it turns up on top of the washing machine where you left it when you threw some stuff in the dryer); your glasses (in their black case on the black mat on the floor of the car where you dropped them when you came home the night before); your socks (in the sock drawer where they belong but it turns out you opened the wrong drawer); your underwear (still in the dryer).

I suppose when we're very old and the children are grown and I have retired from my job and you're home all day, I'll be glad to have the chance to find your things and look after you... BUT I DON'T THINK SO!

Don't Forget where these go...

Money

Keys

Credit Cards

Wallet & ID

Underwear

Socks

A FINAL THOUGHT...

I hope you understand that I love you very much and I wrote this manual to make your life easier. When I see that totally confused look on your face when you can't find your wallet that you were holding only ten minutes ago, and when I realize that you have no idea that I've been putting things in the same place since we were married, and when I go to the bathroom and see an empty cardboard roll on the toilet paper holder, and when I come home from a trip and see that my children are all wearing each other's clothes, I do wonder how you got through Harvard—not to mention Harvard Law School. But I still love you.

What I was trying to get through to you was that I wasn't born knowing how to do all this boring stuff. And my mother didn't give me lessons on how to cook and clean and wash dishes and soothe crying babies and stuff little boys into snowsuits and answer the phone. When I married you, there seemed to be this unwritten agreement that all the crappy stuff would be my responsibility and all the lofty intellectual stuff was yours. Hey, I was a political science major. They don't teach supermarket shopping with three small boys in any of those classes. I have an actual brain. It's as good as yours. But I love you anyway.

And I love your mother. She's a fantastic woman. Brilliant. Wonderful to talk to. One of the early feminists who was determined to bring up her sons with the same sensitivity and love of cooking and cleaning up after himself that she taught her daughter. After all, she was a pediatrician who needed her children to help her with the household crap. We've talked about this many times because I want to bring up my sons with the innate sense of doing what needs to be done in a house without being told. The first time I talked to her about this she smiled at me pityingly and said, "Oh my dear, that gene is left out of boys." And she's a feminist. And a doctor. And a believer.

All I ask is that you think to yourself sometimes: "If I leave this piece of paper here on the table, or this jar of jam on the counter, or my underwear on the floor, or the car without gas, or my Kleenex on the chair, who is going to pick it up?" Think. There's only one other person in your life who has to put all those things where they belong. And that person is not the maid, because we don't have one. And it's not your mother, because she lives in another state. And it's not one of your children, because they're all boys. The only person left to pick up all these things is ME. Your loving, intelligent, resentful wife.

There was a *New Yorker* cartoon last week that made me laugh and cry at the same time. A husband and wife were sitting at the breakfast table and the wife said, "Pass the salt! Pass the salt! What am I—your slave?" I know you don't think of me as your slave. But I wish you'd try to think of me as your partner. Oh, and did I mention—I love you.